Oceanic Eats

A Seafood Salad Cookbook

OCEANIC EATS

First edition. April 5, 2024.

ISBN: 979-8224117598

Written by Jose Maria.

Table of Contents

Oceanic Eats 1

Chapter (1) Classic Seafood Salads 5

Chapter (2) Regional Seafood Salad Varieties....................... 10

Chapter (3) Creative Twists on Seafood Salads 14

Chapter (4) Vegetarian Seafood Alternatives 18

Chapter (5) Dressings and Sauces....................................... 22

Chapter (6) Side Dishes and Accompaniments..................... 25

Chapter (7) Tips for Perfect Seafood Salads 28

Chapter (8) Serving Suggestions and Occasions 30

Chapter (9) Seafood Salad Bowls.. 32

Chapter (10) Seafood Pasta Salads 36

Chapter (11) Seafood Salad Wraps and Rolls 40

Chapter (12) Seafood Salad Appetizers................................ 44

Chapter (13) Seafood Salad for Breakfast............................ 48

Chapter (14) Seafood Salad for Kids 53

Chapter (15) Seafood Salad for Special Diets....................... 56

Chapter (16) Seafood Salad for Entertaining........................ 60

Chapter (17) Seafood Salad Dressing DIY 64

Chapter (18) Seafood Salad Preservation and Canning 67

Chapter (19) Seafood Salad Garnishes and Toppings...................... 71

Chapter (20) Seafood Salad and Wine Pairings 74

Jose Maria

❖ Introduction to Seafood Salads

A. Brief History of Seafood Salads

Seafood salads have a rich history spanning various cultures and culinary traditions. The concept of combining seafood with fresh greens and flavorful dressings dates back centuries, with each region contributing its own unique twists to the dish.

In ancient times, seafood salads were enjoyed by coastal communities around the world, who made use of the abundant seafood available to them. The Greeks and Romans, for example, often incorporated fish and shellfish into their salads, seasoned with olive oil, vinegar, and herbs.

During the Renaissance period, seafood salads gained popularity among European nobility as a symbol of luxury and refinement. Exotic ingredients such as lobster, crab, and shrimp were prized delicacies reserved for special occasions.

In the 20th century, seafood salads became more accessible to the masses as transportation and refrigeration improved, allowing for the distribution of fresh seafood to inland regions. This led to the development of iconic dishes like the Crab Louie Salad in the United States and the Tuna Nicoise Salad in France.

Today, seafood salads continue to evolve, with chefs and home cooks experimenting with new flavors, ingredients, and presentations. From classic recipes to innovative creations, seafood salads remain a beloved dish enjoyed by people around the world.

B. Health Benefits of Seafood

Seafood is not only delicious but also packed with essential nutrients that promote overall health and well-being. Incorporating seafood into your diet can offer a wide range of health benefits, including:

A. Omega-3 Fatty Acids: Seafood is one of the best sources of omega-3 fatty acids, which are essential for heart health. Omega-3s help lower blood pressure, reduce inflammation, and decrease the risk of heart disease.

B. Protein: Seafood is a lean source of high-quality protein, which is essential for muscle growth and repair. Protein also helps keep you feeling full and satisfied, making it a great option for weight management.

C. Vitamins and Minerals: Seafood is rich in vitamins and minerals, including vitamin D, vitamin B12, iodine, and selenium. These nutrients play key roles in bone health, immune function, thyroid health, and more.

D. Low in Saturated Fat: Compared to other animal proteins, seafood is generally low in saturated fat, making it a heart-healthy choice.

E. Brain Health: Omega-3 fatty acids found in seafood are important for brain development and function, and may help reduce the risk of cognitive decline and Alzheimer's disease.

By incorporating a variety of seafood into your diet, you can enjoy these health benefits while savoring delicious and nutritious meals.

C. Essential Ingredients and Tools

To create delicious seafood salads at home, it's important to have a few essential ingredients and tools on hand:

Ingredients:

1. Fresh Seafood (such as shrimp, tuna, crab, salmon, scallops, etc.)
2. Fresh Greens (such as lettuce, spinach, arugula, kale, etc.)
3. Vegetables (such as tomatoes, cucumbers, bell peppers, onions, etc.)
4. Fresh Herbs (such as parsley, dill, cilantro, basil, etc.)
5. Citrus (such as lemon, lime, or orange)
6. Olive Oil and Vinegar (for dressings)
7. Seasonings and Spices (such as salt, pepper, garlic powder, etc.)
8. Optional Add-ins (such as avocado, mango, nuts, seeds, etc.)

Tools:

1. Chef's Knife and Cutting Board
2. Mixing Bowls
3. Whisk or Fork (for mixing dressings)
4. Salad Spinner (for washing and drying greens)
5. Tongs or Salad Servers
6. Serving Plates or Bowls
7. Optional: Grill or Skillet (for cooking seafood)
8. Optional: Blender or Food Processor (for making creamy dressings)

With these ingredients and tools, you'll be well-equipped to whip up a variety of delicious seafood salads to enjoy with family and friends.

Chapter (1) Classic Seafood Salads

A. Shrimp Caesar Salad
Ingredients:

- 1 lb (450g) large shrimp, peeled and deveined
- 1 tablespoon olive oil
- Salt and pepper, to taste
- 1 head romaine lettuce, washed and chopped
- 1 cup croutons
- 1/2 cup grated Parmesan cheese

Caesar Dressing:

- 1/4 cup mayonnaise
- 2 tablespoons grated Parmesan cheese
- 1 tablespoon lemon juice
- 1 teaspoon Dijon mustard
- 1 garlic clove, minced
- Salt and pepper, to taste

Instructions:

1. Preheat a skillet over medium heat. Season the shrimp with olive oil, salt, and pepper. Cook the shrimp in the skillet until pink and cooked through, about 2-3 minutes per side. Remove from heat and set aside.
2. In a large bowl, toss the chopped romaine lettuce with the croutons and grated Parmesan cheese.
3. In a small bowl, whisk together all the ingredients for the Caesar dressing until smooth and well combined.
4. Pour the Caesar dressing over the lettuce mixture and toss until evenly coated.

5. Divide the salad among serving plates and top with the cooked shrimp. Serve immediately, garnished with additional Parmesan cheese if desired.

B. Tuna Nicoise Salad
Ingredients:

- 1 lb (450g) fresh tuna steak
- 1 tablespoon olive oil
- Salt and pepper, to taste
- 4 cups mixed salad greens
- 1 cup cherry tomatoes, halved
- 1/2 cup Niçoise olives
- 4 hard-boiled eggs, peeled and halved
- 1/4 cup capers
- 4 anchovy fillets (optional)

Vinaigrette:

- 1/4 cup olive oil
- 2 tablespoons red wine vinegar
- 1 tablespoon Dijon mustard
- 1 garlic clove, minced
- Salt and pepper, to taste

Instructions:

1. Preheat a grill or skillet over medium-high heat. Season the tuna steak with olive oil, salt, and pepper. Grill or sear the tuna steak for 2-3 minutes per side, or until desired doneness. Remove from heat and let it rest for a few minutes before slicing.
2. In a large bowl, arrange the mixed salad greens, cherry tomatoes, Niçoise olives, hard-boiled eggs, capers, and anchovy fillets (if using).

3. In a small bowl, whisk together the olive oil, red wine vinegar, Dijon mustard, minced garlic, salt, and pepper to make the vinaigrette.
4. Drizzle the vinaigrette over the salad and toss gently to combine.
5. Slice the grilled tuna steak and arrange it on top of the salad. Serve immediately, with extra vinaigrette on the side if desired.

C. Crab Louie Salad

Ingredients:

- 1 lb (450g) lump crab meat
- 4 cups mixed salad greens
- 1 cup cherry tomatoes, halved
- 1/2 cup sliced cucumber
- 1/4 cup sliced red onion
- 4 hard-boiled eggs, peeled and quartered
- Lemon wedges, for serving

Louie Dressing:

- 1/2 cup mayonnaise
- 2 tablespoons ketchup
- 2 tablespoons sweet pickle relish
- 1 tablespoon Worcestershire sauce
- 1 teaspoon hot sauce (optional)
- Salt and pepper, to taste

Instructions:

1. In a large bowl, combine the lump crab meat, mixed salad greens, cherry tomatoes, sliced cucumber, and sliced red onion.
2. In a small bowl, whisk together the mayonnaise, ketchup, sweet pickle relish, Worcestershire sauce, hot sauce (if using), salt, and

pepper to make the Louie dressing.

3. Pour the dressing over the salad and toss gently to coat.
4. Divide the salad among serving plates and top each plate with quartered hard-boiled eggs.
5. Serve immediately, with lemon wedges on the side for squeezing over the salad.

D. Smoked Salmon Salad
Ingredients:

- 8 oz (225g) smoked salmon, thinly sliced
- 4 cups mixed salad greens
- 1 cup cherry tomatoes, halved
- 1/2 cup sliced cucumber
- 1/4 cup sliced red onion
- 1/4 cup chopped fresh dill

Creamy Dill Dressing:

- 1/2 cup sour cream
- 2 tablespoons mayonnaise
- 2 tablespoons chopped fresh dill
- 1 tablespoon lemon juice
- 1 garlic clove, minced
- Salt and pepper, to taste

Instructions:

1. In a large bowl, combine the smoked salmon, mixed salad greens, cherry tomatoes, sliced cucumber, sliced red onion, and chopped fresh dill.
2. In a small bowl, whisk together the sour cream, mayonnaise, chopped fresh dill, lemon juice, minced garlic, salt, and pepper to make the creamy dill dressing.

3. Pour the dressing over the salad and toss gently to coat.
4. Divide the salad among serving plates and serve immediately.

These classic seafood salads are perfect for any occasion, whether you're hosting a dinner party or enjoying a light lunch at home. Enjoy the fresh flavors of shrimp, tuna, crab, and smoked salmon in these delicious and nutritious salads!

Chapter (2) Regional Seafood Salad Varieties

A. Mediterranean Seafood Salad

Ingredients:

- 1 lb (450g) mixed seafood (such as shrimp, calamari, and mussels), cleaned and cooked
- 4 cups mixed salad greens
- 1 cup cherry tomatoes, halved
- 1/2 cup sliced cucumber
- 1/4 cup sliced red onion
- 1/4 cup Kalamata olives
- 2 tablespoons chopped fresh parsley
- 2 tablespoons chopped fresh basil
- Lemon wedges, for serving

Mediterranean Dressing:

- 1/4 cup extra virgin olive oil
- 2 tablespoons red wine vinegar
- 1 garlic clove, minced
- 1 teaspoon dried oregano
- Salt and pepper, to taste

Instructions:

1. In a large bowl, combine the cooked mixed seafood, mixed salad greens, cherry tomatoes, sliced cucumber, sliced red onion, Kalamata olives, chopped fresh parsley, and chopped fresh basil.
2. In a small bowl, whisk together the extra virgin olive oil, red wine vinegar, minced garlic, dried oregano, salt, and pepper to make the Mediterranean dressing.

3. Pour the dressing over the salad and toss gently to coat.
4. Divide the salad among serving plates and serve immediately, with lemon wedges on the side for squeezing over the salad.

B. Thai Seafood Salad
Ingredients:

- 1 lb (450g) mixed seafood (such as shrimp, squid, and scallops), cleaned and cooked
- 4 cups mixed salad greens
- 1 cup shredded cabbage
- 1/2 cup shredded carrots
- 1/4 cup chopped fresh cilantro
- 1/4 cup chopped fresh mint
- 1/4 cup chopped peanuts
- Lime wedges, for serving

Thai Dressing:

- 1/4 cup fish sauce
- 2 tablespoons lime juice
- 1 tablespoon soy sauce
- 1 tablespoon brown sugar
- 1 garlic clove, minced
- 1 Thai chili, finely chopped (optional)

Instructions:

1. In a large bowl, combine the cooked mixed seafood, mixed salad greens, shredded cabbage, shredded carrots, chopped fresh cilantro, chopped fresh mint, and chopped peanuts.
2. In a small bowl, whisk together the fish sauce, lime juice, soy sauce, brown sugar, minced garlic, and chopped Thai chili (if using) to make the Thai dressing.

3. Pour the dressing over the salad and toss gently to coat.
4. Divide the salad among serving plates and serve immediately, with lime wedges on the side for squeezing over the salad.

C. Caribbean Conch Salad
Ingredients:

- 1 lb (450g) conch meat, thinly sliced
- 1 cup diced tomato
- 1/2 cup diced onion
- 1/2 cup diced bell pepper
- 1/4 cup chopped fresh cilantro
- 1/4 cup chopped fresh parsley
- 1/4 cup lime juice
- 2 tablespoons orange juice
- 1 tablespoon olive oil
- Salt and pepper, to taste

Instructions:

1. In a large bowl, combine the thinly sliced conch meat, diced tomato, diced onion, diced bell pepper, chopped fresh cilantro, and chopped fresh parsley.
2. In a small bowl, whisk together the lime juice, orange juice, olive oil, salt, and pepper to make the dressing.
3. Pour the dressing over the salad and toss gently to coat.
4. Cover the bowl and refrigerate the salad for at least 30 minutes to allow the flavors to meld together.
5. Serve the Caribbean conch salad chilled, garnished with additional chopped cilantro and parsley if desired.

D. Japanese Seaweed Salad
Ingredients:

- 4 cups mixed seaweed (such as wakame and hijiki), rehydrated if dried
- 1/4 cup rice vinegar
- 2 tablespoons soy sauce
- 1 tablespoon sesame oil
- 1 tablespoon honey or sugar
- 1 teaspoon grated ginger
- 1 teaspoon sesame seeds
- 1/4 cup sliced cucumber
- 1/4 cup sliced radish
- 1/4 cup shredded carrot
- 1/4 cup sliced green onion

Instructions:

1. In a large bowl, combine the rehydrated mixed seaweed, sliced cucumber, sliced radish, shredded carrot, and sliced green onion.
2. In a small bowl, whisk together the rice vinegar, soy sauce, sesame oil, honey or sugar, grated ginger, and sesame seeds to make the dressing.
3. Pour the dressing over the seaweed salad and toss gently to coat.
4. Cover the bowl and refrigerate the salad for at least 30 minutes to allow the flavors to meld together.
5. Serve the Japanese seaweed salad chilled, garnished with additional sesame seeds and sliced green onion if desired.

These regional seafood salads showcase the diverse flavors and ingredients found around the world, from the Mediterranean to the Caribbean to Japan. Enjoy the vibrant and refreshing flavors of these unique salads!

Chapter (3) Creative Twists on Seafood Salads

A. Grilled Scallop and Mango Salad
  Ingredients:

- 1 lb (450g) fresh scallops
- 1 ripe mango, peeled and diced
- 4 cups mixed salad greens
- 1/4 cup sliced red onion
- 1/4 cup chopped fresh cilantro
- 1/4 cup chopped fresh mint
- 2 tablespoons olive oil
- 2 tablespoons lime juice
- Salt and pepper, to taste

Instructions:

1. Preheat a grill or grill pan over medium-high heat. Season the scallops with olive oil, salt, and pepper. Grill the scallops for 2-3 minutes per side, or until cooked through and lightly charred. Remove from heat and let them cool slightly.
2. In a large bowl, combine the diced mango, mixed salad greens, sliced red onion, chopped fresh cilantro, and chopped fresh mint.
3. In a small bowl, whisk together the olive oil and lime juice to make the dressing. Season with salt and pepper to taste.
4. Slice the grilled scallops and add them to the salad.
5. Drizzle the dressing over the salad and toss gently to coat.
6. Divide the salad among serving plates and serve immediately, garnished with additional chopped cilantro and mint if desired.

B. Avocado and Lobster Salad

Ingredients:

- 1 lb (450g) cooked lobster meat, chopped
- 2 ripe avocados, diced
- 4 cups mixed salad greens
- 1/4 cup diced red bell pepper
- 1/4 cup diced cucumber
- 1/4 cup chopped fresh chives
- 2 tablespoons olive oil
- 2 tablespoons lemon juice
- Salt and pepper, to taste

Instructions:

1. In a large bowl, combine the chopped lobster meat, diced avocados, mixed salad greens, diced red bell pepper, diced cucumber, and chopped fresh chives.
2. In a small bowl, whisk together the olive oil and lemon juice to make the dressing. Season with salt and pepper to taste.
3. Drizzle the dressing over the salad and toss gently to coat.
4. Divide the salad among serving plates and serve immediately.

C. Cajun Blackened Catfish Salad
Ingredients:

- 1 lb (450g) catfish fillets
- 2 tablespoons Cajun seasoning
- 4 cups mixed salad greens
- 1/2 cup sliced cherry tomatoes
- 1/4 cup sliced red onion
- 1/4 cup sliced bell pepper
- 2 tablespoons olive oil
- 2 tablespoons balsamic vinegar
- Salt and pepper, to taste

Instructions:

1. Preheat a skillet over medium-high heat. Season the catfish fillets with Cajun seasoning on both sides.
2. Cook the catfish fillets in the skillet for 3-4 minutes per side, or until blackened and cooked through. Remove from heat and let them cool slightly.
3. In a large bowl, combine the mixed salad greens, sliced cherry tomatoes, sliced red onion, and sliced bell pepper.
4. In a small bowl, whisk together the olive oil and balsamic vinegar to make the dressing. Season with salt and pepper to taste.
5. Break the blackened catfish fillets into bite-sized pieces and add them to the salad.
6. Drizzle the dressing over the salad and toss gently to coat.
7. Divide the salad among serving plates and serve immediately.

D. Spicy Octopus and Cucumber Salad

Ingredients:

- 1 lb (450g) cooked octopus, sliced
- 1 cucumber, thinly sliced
- 4 cups mixed salad greens
- 1/4 cup sliced red onion
- 1/4 cup chopped fresh cilantro
- 1/4 cup chopped fresh mint
- 2 tablespoons olive oil
- 2 tablespoons rice vinegar
- 1 teaspoon sriracha sauce (adjust to taste)
- Salt and pepper, to taste

Instructions:

1. In a large bowl, combine the sliced octopus, thinly sliced

cucumber, mixed salad greens, sliced red onion, chopped fresh cilantro, and chopped fresh mint.

2. In a small bowl, whisk together the olive oil, rice vinegar, and sriracha sauce to make the dressing. Season with salt and pepper to taste.
3. Drizzle the dressing over the salad and toss gently to coat.
4. Divide the salad among serving plates and serve immediately.

These creative twists on seafood salads offer unique flavor combinations and vibrant presentations that are sure to impress. Enjoy the fresh and delicious taste of grilled scallops, lobster, blackened catfish, and spicy octopus in these innovative salads!

Chapter (4) Vegetarian Seafood Alternatives

A. Hearts of Palm "Crab" Salad
Ingredients:

- 1 can (14 oz/400g) hearts of palm, drained and sliced
- 1/4 cup diced red bell pepper
- 1/4 cup diced celery
- 2 tablespoons chopped fresh parsley
- 2 tablespoons chopped fresh chives
- 2 tablespoons vegan mayonnaise
- 1 tablespoon Dijon mustard
- 1 tablespoon lemon juice
- Salt and pepper, to taste
- Lettuce leaves, for serving

Instructions:

1. In a large bowl, combine the sliced hearts of palm, diced red bell pepper, diced celery, chopped fresh parsley, and chopped fresh chives.
2. In a small bowl, whisk together the vegan mayonnaise, Dijon mustard, lemon juice, salt, and pepper to make the dressing.
3. Pour the dressing over the hearts of palm mixture and toss gently to coat.
4. Serve the hearts of palm "crab" salad on lettuce leaves, garnished with additional chopped parsley and chives if desired.

B. Vegan "Tuna" Salad (made with chickpeas)
Ingredients:

- 1 can (15 oz/425g) chickpeas, drained and rinsed
- 1/4 cup diced red onion
- 1/4 cup diced celery
- 2 tablespoons chopped fresh parsley
- 2 tablespoons vegan mayonnaise
- 1 tablespoon lemon juice
- 1 teaspoon Dijon mustard
- Salt and pepper, to taste
- Bread or lettuce leaves, for serving

Instructions:

1. In a large bowl, mash the chickpeas with a fork or potato masher until they reach a chunky consistency.
2. Add the diced red onion, diced celery, chopped fresh parsley, vegan mayonnaise, lemon juice, Dijon mustard, salt, and pepper to the mashed chickpeas. Stir until well combined.
3. Serve the vegan "tuna" salad on bread as a sandwich filling or on lettuce leaves as a salad wrap.

C. Seaweed and Edamame Salad

Ingredients:

- 2 cups cooked and cooled edamame
- 1 cup rehydrated wakame seaweed, drained
- 1/4 cup sliced cucumber
- 1/4 cup shredded carrot
- 2 tablespoons rice vinegar
- 1 tablespoon soy sauce
- 1 tablespoon sesame oil
- 1 teaspoon grated ginger
- 1 teaspoon sesame seeds

Instructions:

1. In a large bowl, combine the cooked and cooled edamame, rehydrated wakame seaweed, sliced cucumber, and shredded carrot.
2. In a small bowl, whisk together the rice vinegar, soy sauce, sesame oil, and grated ginger to make the dressing.
3. Pour the dressing over the salad and toss gently to coat.
4. Sprinkle the salad with sesame seeds before serving.

D. Jackfruit "Shrimp" Salad
Ingredients:

- 1 can (20 oz/565g) young green jackfruit in brine, drained and rinsed
- 1/4 cup diced red onion
- 1/4 cup diced celery
- 2 tablespoons chopped fresh parsley
- 2 tablespoons vegan mayonnaise
- 1 tablespoon lemon juice
- 1 teaspoon Old Bay seasoning (optional)
- Salt and pepper, to taste
- Lettuce leaves, for serving

Instructions:

1. Shred the jackfruit using your fingers or a fork to resemble the texture of shredded shrimp.
2. In a large bowl, combine the shredded jackfruit, diced red onion, diced celery, chopped fresh parsley, vegan mayonnaise, lemon juice, Old Bay seasoning (if using), salt, and pepper.
3. Toss the ingredients until well combined.
4. Serve the jackfruit "shrimp" salad on lettuce leaves, garnished with additional chopped parsley if desired.

These vegetarian seafood alternatives offer delicious and nutritious options for those looking to enjoy the flavors of seafood in a plant-based form. Enjoy the heartiness of hearts of palm, chickpeas, seaweed, and jackfruit in these creative and flavorful salads!

Chapter (5) Dressings and Sauces

A. Classic Lemon-Dill Vinaigrette
Ingredients:

- 1/4 cup extra virgin olive oil
- 2 tablespoons lemon juice
- 1 tablespoon finely chopped fresh dill
- 1 teaspoon Dijon mustard
- 1 teaspoon honey or maple syrup
- Salt and pepper, to taste

Instructions:

1. In a small bowl, whisk together the extra virgin olive oil, lemon juice, finely chopped fresh dill, Dijon mustard, honey or maple syrup, salt, and pepper until well combined.
2. Taste and adjust the seasoning, adding more salt and pepper if needed.
3. Use immediately or store in an airtight container in the refrigerator for up to one week. Before using, let it come to room temperature and give it a good shake or whisk to re-emulsify.

B. Spicy Sriracha Mayo
Ingredients:

- 1/2 cup vegan mayonnaise or regular mayonnaise
- 1 tablespoon sriracha sauce (adjust to taste)
- 1 tablespoon lime juice
- 1 teaspoon soy sauce (or tamari for gluten-free option)
- 1 teaspoon honey or maple syrup (optional)
- 1 teaspoon sesame oil (optional)

Instructions:

1. In a small bowl, whisk together the vegan mayonnaise or regular mayonnaise, sriracha sauce, lime juice, soy sauce, honey or maple syrup (if using), and sesame oil (if using) until smooth and well combined.
2. Taste and adjust the seasoning, adding more sriracha sauce for extra spiciness or lime juice for acidity if needed.
3. Use immediately as a dipping sauce or dressing, or store in an airtight container in the refrigerator for up to one week.

C. Creamy Avocado Lime Dressing

Ingredients:

- 1 ripe avocado, peeled and pitted
- 1/4 cup fresh cilantro leaves
- 1/4 cup plain Greek yogurt or vegan yogurt
- 2 tablespoons lime juice
- 1 tablespoon olive oil
- 1 garlic clove, minced
- Salt and pepper, to taste
- Water (as needed to thin out the dressing)

Instructions:

1. In a blender or food processor, combine the ripe avocado, fresh cilantro leaves, Greek yogurt or vegan yogurt, lime juice, olive oil, minced garlic, salt, and pepper.
2. Blend until smooth and creamy, adding water as needed to achieve the desired consistency.
3. Taste and adjust the seasoning, adding more salt and pepper if needed.

4. Use immediately as a salad dressing or sauce, or store in an airtight container in the refrigerator for up to two days.

D. Sesame Ginger Soy Sauce
Ingredients:

- 1/4 cup soy sauce or tamari (for gluten-free option)
- 2 tablespoons rice vinegar
- 1 tablespoon sesame oil
- 1 tablespoon finely grated ginger
- 1 garlic clove, minced
- 1 tablespoon honey or maple syrup
- 1 teaspoon sesame seeds
- 1 green onion, thinly sliced (optional)

Instructions:

1. In a small bowl, whisk together the soy sauce or tamari, rice vinegar, sesame oil, finely grated ginger, minced garlic, honey or maple syrup, sesame seeds, and thinly sliced green onion (if using) until well combined.
2. Taste and adjust the seasoning, adding more soy sauce for saltiness or honey for sweetness if needed.
3. Use immediately as a marinade, dipping sauce, or salad dressing, or store in an airtight container in the refrigerator for up to one week.

These versatile dressings and sauces add delicious flavor and flair to your seafood salads. Whether you prefer tangy vinaigrettes, spicy mayo, creamy avocado lime dressing, or savory sesame ginger soy sauce, there's a dressing here to suit every taste preference!

Chapter (6) Side Dishes and Accompaniments

A. Garlic Butter Toast Points
Ingredients:

- 1 French baguette, sliced into 1/2-inch thick slices
- 4 tablespoons unsalted butter, softened
- 2 garlic cloves, minced
- 2 tablespoons chopped fresh parsley
- Salt, to taste

Instructions:

1. Preheat the oven to 375°F (190°C). Arrange the baguette slices in a single layer on a baking sheet.
2. In a small bowl, mix together the softened butter, minced garlic, chopped fresh parsley, and salt until well combined.
3. Spread a generous amount of the garlic butter mixture onto each baguette slice.
4. Bake in the preheated oven for 10-12 minutes, or until the toast points are golden brown and crispy.
5. Remove from the oven and let them cool slightly before serving.

B. Crispy Wonton Strips
Ingredients:

- 10 wonton wrappers, cut into thin strips
- Vegetable oil, for frying
- Salt, to taste

Instructions:

1. Heat vegetable oil in a deep fryer or large skillet to 350°F (175°C).
2. Carefully add the wonton strips in batches to the hot oil, frying until golden brown and crispy, about 1-2 minutes.
3. Use a slotted spoon to transfer the crispy wonton strips to a paper towel-lined plate to drain excess oil.
4. Sprinkle with salt while still warm.
5. Allow to cool slightly before serving. These strips can be stored in an airtight container for up to 2 days.

C. Herb-infused Quinoa
Ingredients:

- 1 cup quinoa, rinsed and drained
- 2 cups vegetable broth or water
- 2 tablespoons chopped fresh herbs (such as parsley, cilantro, or basil)
- Salt and pepper, to taste

Instructions:

1. In a medium saucepan, bring the vegetable broth or water to a boil. Stir in the quinoa and reduce heat to low. Cover and simmer for 15-20 minutes, or until the quinoa is cooked and the liquid is absorbed.
2. Remove from heat and let the quinoa sit, covered, for 5 minutes.
3. Fluff the quinoa with a fork and stir in the chopped fresh herbs.
4. Season with salt and pepper to taste.
5. Serve the herb-infused quinoa as a side dish alongside your seafood salads.

D. Seared Sourdough Crostini
Ingredients:

- 1 loaf sourdough bread, sliced into 1/2-inch thick slices
- 2 tablespoons olive oil
- Salt and pepper, to taste

Instructions:

1. Preheat a grill pan or skillet over medium-high heat.
2. Brush both sides of the sourdough bread slices with olive oil and season with salt and pepper.
3. Working in batches, place the bread slices in the preheated pan and cook for 1-2 minutes on each side, or until lightly golden brown and crispy.
4. Remove from heat and let the crostini cool slightly before serving.
5. Serve alongside your seafood salads as a delicious crunchy accompaniment.

These side dishes and accompaniments complement your seafood salads perfectly, offering a variety of textures and flavors to complete your meal. Enjoy the crunch of garlic butter toast points, crispy wonton strips, herb-infused quinoa, and seared sourdough crostini alongside your fresh and flavorful salads!

Chapter (7) Tips for Perfect Seafood Salads

A. Selecting and Preparing Fresh Seafood:

- Freshness is Key: When selecting seafood for your salad, always opt for the freshest options available. Look for firm, shiny flesh with no strong fishy odor.
- Proper Storage: If you're not using the seafood immediately, store it in the refrigerator and use it within a day or two to maintain freshness.
- Safe Handling: Always handle seafood with care and follow proper food safety guidelines to avoid cross-contamination.
- Cooking Methods: Choose cooking methods that enhance the natural flavors of the seafood, such as grilling, steaming, or poaching. Avoid overcooking, as it can result in tough and dry seafood.

B. Balancing Flavors and Textures:

- Variety is Key: Incorporate a variety of flavors and textures into your salad to keep it interesting. Mix crunchy vegetables with tender seafood, and balance savory elements with tangy dressings or citrus flavors.
- Seasoning: Don't forget to season each component of your salad appropriately with salt, pepper, and other herbs and spices to enhance their flavors.
- Acid Balance: Use acidic ingredients like lemon juice or vinegar to brighten up the flavors and cut through the richness of the seafood.

C. Presentation and Garnishing Techniques:

- Visual Appeal: Pay attention to the presentation of your seafood salad. Arrange ingredients neatly on the plate and use vibrant, colorful components to make the dish visually appealing.
- Garnishes: Garnish your salad with fresh herbs, citrus wedges, or additional toppings like toasted nuts or seeds to add texture and flavor.
- Plating Techniques: Experiment with different plating techniques, such as layering ingredients or arranging them in a decorative pattern, to elevate the presentation of your seafood salad.

D. Storage and Leftover Ideas:

- Refrigeration: Store leftover seafood salad in an airtight container in the refrigerator for up to 2-3 days. Make sure to consume it within this timeframe to ensure freshness.
- Reviving Leftovers: If the salad seems a bit dry after refrigeration, you can refresh it by adding a drizzle of dressing or a squeeze of fresh lemon juice before serving.
- Creative Reuse: Transform leftover seafood salad into new dishes by incorporating it into sandwiches, wraps, or pasta salads. You can also use it as a topping for baked potatoes or as a filling for stuffed vegetables.

By following these tips, you can create delicious and satisfying seafood salads that are bursting with flavor, texture, and visual appeal. Enjoy experimenting with different ingredients and techniques to customize your salads to suit your taste preferences!

Chapter (8) Serving Suggestions and Occasions

A. Picnics and Outdoor Gatherings:

- Portable Options: Opt for seafood salads that are easy to transport and serve outdoors, such as Mediterranean Seafood Salad or Thai Seafood Salad.
- Packaging: Use leak-proof containers or sealable bags to keep the salads fresh during transportation. Consider packing individual portions for convenience.
- Accompaniments: Pair the seafood salads with portable side dishes like crispy wonton strips or seared sourdough crostini for added crunch.

B. Elegant Dinner Parties:

- Sophisticated Presentation: Showcase your seafood salads in elegant serving dishes and garnish them with fresh herbs or edible flowers for a refined touch.
- Plated Service: Serve individual portions of seafood salad on chilled salad plates for an upscale dining experience.
- Pairing Suggestions: Accompany the salads with a selection of fine wines or champagne to complement the flavors and elevate the dining experience.

C. Quick Weeknight Dinners:

- Efficient Preparation: Choose seafood salads that can be prepared in advance or come together quickly, such as Vegan "Tuna" Salad or Jackfruit "Shrimp" Salad.
- One-Dish Meals: Make the salads more substantial by adding hearty ingredients like quinoa or chickpeas to create a complete

meal.

- Time-Saving Tips: Utilize pre-cooked seafood or pre-prepared ingredients to streamline the cooking process and minimize prep time.

D. Light and Refreshing Summer Meals:

- Seasonal Ingredients: Take advantage of fresh, seasonal produce like cucumbers, tomatoes, and herbs to create light and refreshing seafood salads.
- Chilled Options: Serve the salads chilled or at room temperature to combat the heat and provide a refreshing dining experience.
- Al Fresco Dining: Enjoy the seafood salads outdoors on a patio or terrace, paired with a crisp white wine or citrus-infused cocktail for a quintessential summer meal.

Whether you're hosting a casual picnic, an elegant dinner party, a busy weeknight meal, or a laid-back summer gathering, there's a perfect seafood salad option to suit the occasion. With the right selection of dishes and serving suggestions, you can create memorable dining experiences for any event or gathering.

Chapter (9) Seafood Salad Bowls

A. Ahi Poke Bowl
Ingredients:

- 1 lb (450g) sushi-grade ahi tuna, cubed
- 2 tablespoons soy sauce
- 1 tablespoon sesame oil
- 1 tablespoon rice vinegar
- 1 teaspoon sriracha sauce (optional)
- 2 cups cooked sushi rice, cooled
- 1 avocado, sliced
- 1/2 cup sliced cucumber
- 1/4 cup sliced radishes
- 1/4 cup sliced green onions
- Sesame seeds, for garnish
- Nori strips, for garnish
- Pickled ginger, for serving
- Wasabi, for serving

Instructions:

1. In a bowl, combine the cubed ahi tuna, soy sauce, sesame oil, rice vinegar, and sriracha sauce (if using). Toss gently to coat the tuna evenly. Marinate in the refrigerator for at least 15 minutes.
2. To assemble the poke bowl, divide the cooked sushi rice among serving bowls. Top with marinated ahi tuna, sliced avocado, sliced cucumber, sliced radishes, and sliced green onions.
3. Garnish with sesame seeds and nori strips.
4. Serve the poke bowls with pickled ginger and wasabi on the side. Enjoy!

B. Seafood Cobb Salad Bowl

Ingredients:

- 1 lb (450g) cooked and chilled shrimp, peeled and deveined
- 4 cups chopped romaine lettuce
- 1 cup cherry tomatoes, halved
- 1 cup cooked and chopped bacon
- 1 avocado, diced
- 1/2 cup crumbled blue cheese
- 2 hard-boiled eggs, sliced
- 1/4 cup sliced green onions
- Ranch dressing, for serving

Instructions:

1. In a large bowl, combine the chopped romaine lettuce, halved cherry tomatoes, chopped bacon, diced avocado, crumbled blue cheese, sliced hard-boiled eggs, and sliced green onions.
2. Toss the salad ingredients gently to combine.
3. Divide the salad among serving bowls.
4. Top each salad bowl with cooked and chilled shrimp.
5. Serve the seafood cobb salad bowls with ranch dressing on the side. Enjoy!

C. Mediterranean Couscous Seafood Bowl

Ingredients:

- 1 cup couscous, cooked according to package instructions and cooled
- 1 lb (450g) cooked and chilled mixed seafood (such as shrimp, calamari, and mussels)
- 1 cup cherry tomatoes, halved
- 1/2 cup sliced cucumber
- 1/4 cup sliced red onion
- 1/4 cup Kalamata olives

- 2 tablespoons chopped fresh parsley
- 2 tablespoons crumbled feta cheese
- Lemon wedges, for serving
- Greek dressing, for serving

Instructions:

1. In a large bowl, combine the cooked couscous, cooked and chilled mixed seafood, halved cherry tomatoes, sliced cucumber, sliced red onion, Kalamata olives, chopped fresh parsley, and crumbled feta cheese.
2. Toss the ingredients gently to combine.
3. Divide the couscous seafood mixture among serving bowls.
4. Serve the Mediterranean couscous seafood bowls with lemon wedges and Greek dressing on the side. Enjoy!

D. Thai Glass Noodle Seafood Bowl
Ingredients:

- 4 oz (113g) dried glass noodles, soaked in hot water until softened and drained
- 1 lb (450g) cooked and chilled mixed seafood (such as shrimp, squid, and scallops)
- 1 cup shredded cabbage
- 1/2 cup shredded carrots
- 1/4 cup chopped fresh cilantro
- 1/4 cup chopped fresh mint
- 1/4 cup chopped peanuts
- Lime wedges, for serving
- Thai dressing (recipe from previous section), for serving

Instructions:

1. In a large bowl, combine the soaked and drained glass noodles,

cooked and chilled mixed seafood, shredded cabbage, shredded carrots, chopped fresh cilantro, chopped fresh mint, and chopped peanuts.
2. Toss the ingredients gently to combine.
3. Divide the glass noodle seafood mixture among serving bowls.
4. Serve the Thai glass noodle seafood bowls with lime wedges and Thai dressing on the side. Enjoy!

These seafood salad bowls offer a delightful fusion of flavors and textures, perfect for a satisfying and nutritious meal. Enjoy the fresh taste of ahi tuna in the poke bowl, the classic combination of shrimp and bacon in the cobb salad bowl, the Mediterranean-inspired couscous seafood bowl, and the vibrant flavors of Thai cuisine in the glass noodle seafood bowl.

Chapter (10) Seafood Pasta Salads

A. Lemon Garlic Shrimp Pasta Salad
Ingredients:

- 8 oz (225g) pasta of your choice (such as fusilli or penne)
- 1 lb (450g) cooked shrimp, peeled and deveined
- 2 cloves garlic, minced
- Zest and juice of 1 lemon
- 2 tablespoons olive oil
- 1 cup cherry tomatoes, halved
- 1/2 cup sliced black olives
- 1/4 cup chopped fresh parsley
- Salt and black pepper, to taste

Instructions:

1. Cook the pasta according to the package instructions until al dente. Drain and rinse under cold water to cool.
2. In a large bowl, combine the cooked shrimp, minced garlic, lemon zest, lemon juice, olive oil, cherry tomatoes, sliced black olives, and chopped fresh parsley.
3. Add the cooked pasta to the bowl and toss gently to combine.
4. Season with salt and black pepper to taste.
5. Serve the lemon garlic shrimp pasta salad chilled or at room temperature. Enjoy!

B. Crab and Avocado Rotini Salad
Ingredients:

- 8 oz (225g) rotini pasta

- 1 lb (450g) lump crabmeat
- 1 avocado, diced
- 1/2 cup diced red bell pepper
- 1/4 cup chopped green onions
- 1/4 cup chopped fresh cilantro
- Juice of 1 lime
- 2 tablespoons olive oil
- Salt and black pepper, to taste

Instructions:

1. Cook the rotini pasta according to the package instructions until al dente. Drain and rinse under cold water to cool.
2. In a large bowl, combine the lump crabmeat, diced avocado, diced red bell pepper, chopped green onions, chopped fresh cilantro, lime juice, and olive oil.
3. Add the cooked rotini pasta to the bowl and toss gently to combine.
4. Season with salt and black pepper to taste.
5. Serve the crab and avocado rotini salad chilled or at room temperature. Enjoy!

C. Tuna and Olive Orzo Salad
Ingredients:

- 8 oz (225g) orzo pasta
- 1 can (5 oz/140g) tuna, drained and flaked
- 1/2 cup sliced black olives
- 1/4 cup chopped sun-dried tomatoes
- 1/4 cup chopped fresh basil
- 2 tablespoons capers
- 2 tablespoons olive oil
- 1 tablespoon red wine vinegar

- Salt and black pepper, to taste

Instructions:

1. Cook the orzo pasta according to the package instructions until al dente. Drain and rinse under cold water to cool.
2. In a large bowl, combine the flaked tuna, sliced black olives, chopped sun-dried tomatoes, chopped fresh basil, capers, olive oil, and red wine vinegar.
3. Add the cooked orzo pasta to the bowl and toss gently to combine.
4. Season with salt and black pepper to taste.
5. Serve the tuna and olive orzo salad chilled or at room temperature. Enjoy!

D. Lobster and Tomato Penne Salad
Ingredients:

- 8 oz (225g) penne pasta
- 1 lb (450g) cooked lobster meat, chopped
- 1 cup cherry tomatoes, halved
- 1/4 cup chopped fresh parsley
- 2 tablespoons chopped fresh chives
- 2 tablespoons olive oil
- 1 tablespoon lemon juice
- Salt and black pepper, to taste

Instructions:

1. Cook the penne pasta according to the package instructions until al dente. Drain and rinse under cold water to cool.
2. In a large bowl, combine the chopped lobster meat, halved cherry tomatoes, chopped fresh parsley, chopped fresh chives, olive oil, and lemon juice.

3. Add the cooked penne pasta to the bowl and toss gently to combine.
4. Season with salt and black pepper to taste.
5. Serve the lobster and tomato penne salad chilled or at room temperature. Enjoy!

These seafood pasta salads offer a delicious and satisfying way to enjoy your favorite seafood in a refreshing and flavorful dish. Whether you prefer the tangy flavors of lemon garlic shrimp, the creamy combination of crab and avocado, the Mediterranean-inspired tuna and olive, or the luxurious lobster and tomato, there's a seafood pasta salad here to suit every taste preference!

Chapter (11) Seafood Salad Wraps and Rolls

A. Lobster Roll Salad Wrap
Ingredients:

- 1 lb (450g) cooked lobster meat, chopped
- 1/4 cup mayonnaise
- 1 tablespoon lemon juice
- 1 celery stalk, finely chopped
- 2 tablespoons chopped fresh chives
- Salt and pepper, to taste
- 4 large lettuce leaves
- 4 large tortillas or wraps

Instructions:

1. In a bowl, combine the chopped lobster meat, mayonnaise, lemon juice, finely chopped celery, chopped fresh chives, salt, and pepper. Mix until well combined.
2. Lay out the lettuce leaves on the tortillas or wraps.
3. Divide the lobster salad mixture among the lettuce leaves.
4. Roll up the wraps, folding in the sides as you go, to enclose the filling.
5. Slice the wraps in half diagonally before serving. Enjoy the lobster roll salad wraps as a delicious handheld meal!

B. Sushi-Inspired Seafood Salad Rolls
Ingredients:

- 1 lb (450g) cooked mixed seafood (such as shrimp, crab, and/or imitation crab), chopped
- 2 tablespoons mayonnaise
- 1 tablespoon sriracha sauce (optional)
- 1 teaspoon soy sauce
- 1 teaspoon rice vinegar
- 1 avocado, thinly sliced
- 1 cucumber, julienned
- 4 sheets nori (seaweed)
- Sushi rice (cooked and seasoned with rice vinegar, sugar, and salt)

Instructions:

1. In a bowl, combine the chopped mixed seafood, mayonnaise, sriracha sauce (if using), soy sauce, and rice vinegar. Mix until well combined.
2. Place a sheet of nori on a bamboo sushi rolling mat.
3. Spread a thin layer of sushi rice over the nori, leaving a small border along the edges.
4. Arrange slices of avocado and julienned cucumber over the rice.
5. Spoon the seafood salad mixture onto the avocado and cucumber.
6. Roll up the nori tightly using the bamboo mat, sealing the edge with a bit of water.
7. Slice the sushi roll into bite-sized pieces using a sharp knife. Repeat with the remaining nori sheets and filling ingredients.
8. Serve the sushi-inspired seafood salad rolls with soy sauce, wasabi, and pickled ginger on the side. Enjoy the delicious flavors reminiscent of sushi in a convenient handheld form!

C. Shrimp and Avocado Nori Wraps
Ingredients:

- 1 lb (450g) cooked shrimp, peeled and deveined
- 1 avocado, sliced
- 1 cucumber, julienned
- 1 carrot, julienned
- 4 sheets nori (seaweed)
- Soy sauce, for dipping

Instructions:

1. Lay out a sheet of nori on a clean, flat surface.
2. Arrange slices of avocado, julienned cucumber, julienned carrot, and cooked shrimp along one edge of the nori sheet.
3. Roll up the nori tightly, enclosing the filling.
4. Use a sharp knife to slice the nori wrap into bite-sized pieces.
5. Serve the shrimp and avocado nori wraps with soy sauce for dipping. Enjoy the refreshing combination of seafood and vegetables wrapped in nori!

D. Crab and Mango Rice Paper Rolls
Ingredients:

- 1 lb (450g) cooked crabmeat, shredded
- 1 ripe mango, thinly sliced
- 1 cucumber, julienned
- 1 carrot, julienned
- 8 rice paper wrappers
- Fresh mint leaves
- Sweet chili sauce, for dipping

Instructions:

1. Fill a shallow dish with warm water. Dip one rice paper wrapper into the water for a few seconds until it becomes pliable.
2. Place the wet rice paper wrapper on a clean, flat surface.
3. Arrange shredded crabmeat, sliced mango, julienned cucumber, julienned carrot, and fresh mint leaves in the center of the rice paper wrapper.
4. Fold the sides of the wrapper over the filling, then roll it up tightly like a burrito.
5. Repeat with the remaining rice paper wrappers and filling ingredients.
6. Serve the crab and mango rice paper rolls with sweet chili sauce for dipping. Enjoy the delightful combination of sweet mango and savory crab wrapped in delicate rice paper!

These seafood salad wraps and rolls offer a convenient and delicious way to enjoy your favorite seafood salads on the go or as a light and refreshing meal. Whether you prefer the classic flavors of a lobster roll salad wrap, the sushi-inspired twist of seafood salad rolls, the simplicity of shrimp and avocado nori wraps, or the tropical flair of crab and mango rice paper rolls, there's a seafood wrap or roll here to satisfy your cravings!

Chapter (12) Seafood Salad Appetizers

A. Scallop Ceviche Cups
   Ingredients:

- 1/2 lb (225g) fresh scallops, thinly sliced
- 1/4 cup lime juice
- 2 tablespoons lemon juice
- 1 small red onion, finely diced
- 1 jalapeño, seeded and minced
- 1/4 cup chopped fresh cilantro
- Salt and pepper, to taste
- Small lettuce cups or endive leaves, for serving
- Avocado slices, for garnish (optional)

Instructions:

1. In a bowl, combine the thinly sliced scallops, lime juice, lemon juice, diced red onion, minced jalapeño, and chopped cilantro. Season with salt and pepper to taste.
2. Cover the bowl and refrigerate for at least 30 minutes to allow the scallops to marinate and "cook" in the citrus juices.
3. When ready to serve, spoon the scallop ceviche mixture into small lettuce cups or endive leaves.
4. Garnish each ceviche cup with a slice of avocado, if desired.
5. Serve immediately as a refreshing and elegant appetizer.

B. Mini Crab Cake Bites
   Ingredients:

- 1 lb (450g) lump crabmeat, picked over for shells

- 1/4 cup mayonnaise
- 1 tablespoon Dijon mustard
- 1 tablespoon Worcestershire sauce
- 1 teaspoon Old Bay seasoning
- 1/4 cup chopped fresh parsley
- 1/4 cup breadcrumbs
- 1 egg, beaten
- Olive oil, for frying
- Lemon wedges, for serving

Instructions:

1. In a bowl, combine the lump crabmeat, mayonnaise, Dijon mustard, Worcestershire sauce, Old Bay seasoning, chopped parsley, breadcrumbs, and beaten egg. Mix until well combined.
2. Shape the crab mixture into small balls or patties.
3. Heat olive oil in a skillet over medium heat. Fry the mini crab cakes until golden brown and crispy on both sides, about 2-3 minutes per side.
4. Drain the crab cakes on paper towels to remove excess oil.
5. Serve the mini crab cake bites hot with lemon wedges on the side for squeezing.

C. Smoked Salmon and Cucumber Bites
Ingredients:

- English cucumber, sliced into rounds
- Smoked salmon slices, cut into smaller pieces
- Cream cheese or goat cheese
- Fresh dill sprigs
- Lemon zest, for garnish

Instructions:

1. Place cucumber rounds on a serving platter.
2. Top each cucumber round with a small piece of smoked salmon.
3. Add a dollop of cream cheese or goat cheese on top of the smoked salmon.
4. Garnish each bite with a sprig of fresh dill and a sprinkle of lemon zest.
5. Serve the smoked salmon and cucumber bites chilled as a refreshing appetizer option.

D. Tuna Tartare Crostini
Ingredients:

- 1/2 lb (225g) sushi-grade tuna, finely diced
- 2 tablespoons soy sauce
- 1 tablespoon sesame oil
- 1 teaspoon rice vinegar
- 1 teaspoon sriracha sauce (optional)
- 1 green onion, thinly sliced
- Sesame seeds, for garnish
- Baguette slices, toasted

Instructions:

1. In a bowl, combine the finely diced tuna, soy sauce, sesame oil, rice vinegar, and sriracha sauce (if using). Mix well to coat the tuna evenly.
2. Spoon the tuna tartare mixture onto toasted baguette slices.
3. Garnish each crostini with thinly sliced green onion and a sprinkle of sesame seeds.
4. Serve the tuna tartare crostini immediately as a sophisticated and flavorful appetizer option.

These seafood salad appetizers offer a delightful array of flavors and textures, perfect for entertaining guests or enjoying as a light starter before a meal. Whether you prefer the bright and tangy Scallop Ceviche Cups, the crispy and savory Mini Crab Cake Bites, the elegant and refreshing Smoked Salmon and Cucumber Bites, or the sophisticated and spicy Tuna Tartare Crostini, there's an appetizer here to suit every taste preference!

Chapter (13) Seafood Salad for Breakfast

A. Smoked Salmon Breakfast Salad
  Ingredients:

- Mixed salad greens
- Smoked salmon slices
- Cherry tomatoes, halved
- Sliced cucumber
- Sliced avocado
- Hard-boiled eggs, sliced
- Red onion, thinly sliced
- Capers
- Lemon wedges
- Olive oil
- Salt and pepper

Instructions:

1. Arrange mixed salad greens on a plate or in a bowl.
2. Top with smoked salmon slices, halved cherry tomatoes, sliced cucumber, sliced avocado, hard-boiled egg slices, and thinly sliced red onion.
3. Sprinkle capers over the salad.
4. Drizzle with olive oil and squeeze lemon wedges over the top.
5. Season with salt and pepper to taste.
6. Enjoy this refreshing and protein-packed breakfast salad!

B. Crab and Asparagus Frittata Salad
  Ingredients:

- Lump crabmeat
- Asparagus spears, trimmed and blanched
- Eggs
- Milk
- Salt and pepper
- Olive oil
- Mixed salad greens
- Lemon vinaigrette

Instructions:

1. Preheat your oven to 375°F (190°C).
2. In a bowl, whisk together eggs, milk, salt, and pepper to make the frittata mixture.
3. Heat olive oil in an oven-safe skillet over medium heat. Add blanched asparagus spears and lump crabmeat.
4. Pour the egg mixture over the crab and asparagus in the skillet. Cook for a few minutes until the edges start to set.
5. Transfer the skillet to the preheated oven and bake for 10-15 minutes or until the frittata is set and golden brown.
6. Let the frittata cool slightly, then cut into wedges.
7. Serve the frittata wedges over a bed of mixed salad greens dressed with lemon vinaigrette.
8. Enjoy this flavorful and satisfying crab and asparagus frittata salad for breakfast!

C. Shrimp and Spinach Omelette Salad
Ingredients:

- Shrimp, peeled and deveined
- Eggs
- Spinach leaves

- Cherry tomatoes, halved
- Red bell pepper, diced
- Red onion, thinly sliced
- Feta cheese, crumbled
- Olive oil
- Salt and pepper

Instructions:

1. In a skillet, heat olive oil over medium heat. Add shrimp and cook until pink and opaque. Remove from the skillet and set aside.
2. In the same skillet, add beaten eggs seasoned with salt and pepper. Cook, gently lifting the edges to allow uncooked eggs to flow underneath, until the omelette is mostly set.
3. Arrange spinach leaves on a plate. Place the omelette on top of the spinach.
4. Top the omelette with cooked shrimp, halved cherry tomatoes, diced red bell pepper, thinly sliced red onion, and crumbled feta cheese.
5. Serve immediately as a delicious and protein-rich breakfast salad.

D. Tuna and Egg Breakfast Bowl
Ingredients:

- Canned tuna, drained
- Hard-boiled eggs, sliced
- Cooked quinoa or brown rice
- Sliced avocado
- Cherry tomatoes, halved
- Cucumber, diced
- Red onion, thinly sliced
- Fresh herbs (such as parsley or cilantro), chopped
- Lemon wedges
- Olive oil
- Salt and pepper

Instructions:

1. In a bowl, combine canned tuna, hard-boiled egg slices, cooked quinoa or brown rice, sliced avocado, halved cherry tomatoes, diced cucumber, thinly sliced red onion, and chopped fresh herbs.
2. Drizzle olive oil over the ingredients and squeeze lemon wedges on top.
3. Season with salt and pepper to taste.
4. Toss gently to combine all the ingredients.
5. Serve the tuna and egg breakfast bowl as a nutritious and filling breakfast option.

These seafood breakfast salads offer a nutritious and delicious start to your day, whether you're looking for something light and refreshing like the Smoked Salmon Breakfast Salad, something hearty and satisfying like the Crab and Asparagus Frittata Salad, something protein-packed like the Shrimp and Spinach Omelette Salad, or something wholesome and nourishing like the Tuna and Egg Breakfast Bowl. Enjoy your seafood breakfast salads to kickstart your morning with flavor and energy!

Chapter (14) Seafood Salad for Kids

A. Fish-shaped Tuna Salad Sandwiches

Ingredients:

- Canned tuna, drained
- Mayonnaise
- Diced celery
- Diced pickles
- Salt and pepper, to taste
- Bread slices
- Fish-shaped cookie cutter
- Lettuce leaves
- Tomato slices (optional)

Instructions:

1. In a bowl, mix canned tuna, mayonnaise, diced celery, diced pickles, salt, and pepper until well combined.
2. Use a fish-shaped cookie cutter to cut out fish-shaped bread slices.
3. Spread tuna salad mixture onto half of the fish-shaped bread slices.
4. Top with lettuce leaves and tomato slices, if desired.
5. Place the remaining fish-shaped bread slices on top to make sandwiches.
6. Serve these fun and nutritious fish-shaped tuna salad sandwiches for a kid-friendly meal or snack.

B. Shrimp and Veggie Pasta Salad Cups

Ingredients:

- Cooked pasta (such as macaroni or fusilli)
- Cooked shrimp, chopped
- Diced cucumbers
- Diced bell peppers (red, yellow, or orange)
- Cherry tomatoes, halved
- Ranch dressing or Italian dressing
- Small plastic cups or muffin cups

Instructions:

1. In a bowl, combine cooked pasta, chopped cooked shrimp, diced cucumbers, diced bell peppers, and halved cherry tomatoes.
2. Add ranch dressing or Italian dressing to the pasta salad and toss until well coated.
3. Spoon the pasta salad into small plastic cups or muffin cups.
4. Serve these shrimp and veggie pasta salad cups as a colorful and tasty meal option for kids.

C. Crab Salad Roll-Ups
Ingredients:

- Canned crabmeat, drained
- Mayonnaise
- Diced celery
- Diced red bell pepper
- Shredded carrots
- Tortillas or wraps
- Lettuce leaves

Instructions:

1. In a bowl, mix canned crabmeat, mayonnaise, diced celery, diced red bell pepper, and shredded carrots until well

combined.

2. Spread the crab salad mixture onto tortillas or wraps.
3. Top with lettuce leaves.
4. Roll up the tortillas or wraps and slice into smaller pieces.
5. Serve these crab salad roll-ups as a tasty and convenient seafood option for kids.

D. Tuna Salad Stuffed Bell Peppers
Ingredients:

- Canned tuna, drained
- Mayonnaise
- Diced celery
- Diced pickles
- Salt and pepper, to taste
- Bell peppers (red, yellow, or orange)

Instructions:

1. In a bowl, mix canned tuna, mayonnaise, diced celery, diced pickles, salt, and pepper until well combined.
2. Cut the tops off bell peppers and remove the seeds and membranes.
3. Stuff the bell peppers with the tuna salad mixture.
4. Serve these tuna salad stuffed bell peppers as a colorful and nutritious meal option for kids.

These seafood salad recipes for kids offer a variety of fun and flavorful options that are sure to appeal to young taste buds. Whether it's the playful Fish-shaped Tuna Salad Sandwiches, the colorful Shrimp and Veggie Pasta Salad Cups, the convenient Crab Salad Roll-Ups, or the nutritious Tuna Salad Stuffed Bell Peppers, there's something here for every child to enjoy!

Chapter (15) Seafood Salad for Special Diets

A. Gluten-Free Crab and Mango Salad

Ingredients:

- Lump crabmeat
- Ripe mango, diced
- Red bell pepper, diced
- Red onion, finely chopped
- Cilantro, chopped
- Lime juice
- Olive oil
- Salt and pepper, to taste
- Mixed salad greens

Instructions:

1. In a bowl, combine lump crabmeat, diced mango, diced red bell pepper, finely chopped red onion, and chopped cilantro.
2. Dress the salad with lime juice and olive oil.
3. Season with salt and pepper to taste.
4. Serve over mixed salad greens for a refreshing and gluten-free seafood salad option.

B. Dairy-Free Shrimp and Avocado Salad

Ingredients:

- Cooked shrimp, peeled and deveined
- Ripe avocado, diced
- Cherry tomatoes, halved
- Red onion, thinly sliced
- Cucumber, diced

- Fresh parsley, chopped
- Lemon juice
- Olive oil
- Salt and pepper, to taste
- Mixed salad greens

Instructions:

1. In a bowl, combine cooked shrimp, diced avocado, halved cherry tomatoes, thinly sliced red onion, diced cucumber, and chopped fresh parsley.
2. Dress the salad with lemon juice and olive oil.
3. Season with salt and pepper to taste.
4. Serve over mixed salad greens for a dairy-free and flavorful seafood salad option.

C. Low-Carb Tuna and Cauliflower Salad
Ingredients:

- Canned tuna, drained
- Cauliflower florets, steamed and chopped
- Celery, diced
- Green onions, sliced
- Dill pickles, diced
- Mayonnaise
- Dijon mustard
- Lemon juice
- Salt and pepper, to taste
- Lettuce leaves

Instructions:

1. In a bowl, combine canned tuna, chopped steamed cauliflower florets, diced celery, sliced green onions, and diced dill pickles.

2. In a separate small bowl, whisk together mayonnaise, Dijon mustard, and lemon juice to make the dressing.
3. Pour the dressing over the tuna mixture and toss until well coated.
4. Season with salt and pepper to taste.
5. Serve the tuna and cauliflower salad over lettuce leaves for a low-carb seafood salad option.

D. Keto-Friendly Salmon and Arugula Salad
Ingredients:

- Grilled or baked salmon fillets, flaked
- Arugula
- Cherry tomatoes, halved
- Cucumber, sliced
- Red onion, thinly sliced
- Avocado, sliced
- Lemon zest
- Lemon juice
- Olive oil
- Salt and pepper, to taste

Instructions:

1. Arrange arugula on a serving platter.
2. Top with flaked grilled or baked salmon fillets, halved cherry tomatoes, sliced cucumber, thinly sliced red onion, and sliced avocado.
3. Drizzle with olive oil and lemon juice.
4. Sprinkle lemon zest over the salad.
5. Season with salt and pepper to taste.
6. Serve this flavorful and keto-friendly salmon and arugula salad as a satisfying seafood salad option.

These seafood salad recipes cater to various dietary restrictions, offering delicious options for those following gluten-free, dairy-free, low-carb, or keto diets. Whether it's the vibrant Gluten-Free Crab and Mango Salad, the creamy Dairy-Free Shrimp and Avocado Salad, the satisfying Low-Carb Tuna and Cauliflower Salad, or the nutrient-packed Keto-Friendly Salmon and Arugula Salad, there's a special diet-friendly seafood salad here for everyone to enjoy!

Chapter (16) Seafood Salad for Entertaining

A. Seafood Charcuterie Board

Ingredients:

- Assorted seafood (such as smoked salmon, cooked shrimp, crab legs, and marinated mussels)
- Assorted cheeses (such as brie, blue cheese, and goat cheese)
- Assorted crackers and breadsticks
- Olives and pickles
- Fresh fruit (such as grapes and berries)
- Nuts (such as almonds and walnuts)
- Honey or jam for drizzling
- Fresh herbs for garnish
- Lemon wedges

Instructions:

1. Arrange the assorted seafood, cheeses, crackers, breadsticks, olives, pickles, fresh fruit, and nuts on a large serving board or platter.
2. Drizzle honey or jam over the cheeses for added sweetness.
3. Garnish with fresh herbs and lemon wedges for extra flavor.
4. Serve the seafood charcuterie board as an impressive and customizable spread for entertaining guests.

B. Seafood Salad Platter with Dipping Sauces
Ingredients:

- Assorted seafood salads (such as shrimp salad, crab salad, and tuna salad)
- Assorted dipping sauces (such as cocktail sauce, tartar sauce, and aioli)
- Mixed salad greens
- Sliced cucumbers and cherry tomatoes
- Lemon wedges
- Fresh herbs for garnish
- Crackers or bread slices

Instructions:

1. Arrange the assorted seafood salads on a large platter, leaving space for dipping sauces.
2. Place small bowls of dipping sauces (cocktail sauce, tartar sauce, and aioli) around the platter.
3. Surround the seafood salads with mixed salad greens, sliced cucumbers, and cherry tomatoes.
4. Garnish with lemon wedges and fresh herbs for an elegant presentation.
5. Serve the seafood salad platter with crackers or bread slices for dipping and enjoying.

C. Seafood Salad Skewers with Citrus Glaze
Ingredients:

- Assorted seafood (such as grilled shrimp, scallops, and salmon cubes)
- Assorted vegetables (such as cherry tomatoes, bell peppers, and zucchini slices)
- Wooden skewers, soaked in water
- Olive oil
- Salt and pepper, to taste
- Citrus glaze (made with orange juice, lemon juice, honey, and soy sauce)
- Fresh herbs for garnish

Instructions:

1. Preheat the grill to medium-high heat.
2. Thread the assorted seafood and vegetables onto the soaked wooden skewers, alternating between seafood and vegetables.
3. Brush the skewers with olive oil and season with salt and pepper.
4. Grill the skewers for 2-3 minutes per side, or until the seafood is cooked through and the vegetables are tender.
5. Brush the grilled skewers with citrus glaze while still hot.
6. Garnish with fresh herbs before serving.
7. Serve the seafood salad skewers with extra citrus glaze on the side for dipping.

D. Seafood Salad Stuffed Mini Bell Peppers
Ingredients:

- Mini bell peppers, halved and deseeded
- Assorted seafood salad fillings (such as crab salad, tuna salad, and shrimp salad)
- Fresh herbs for garnish

Instructions:

1. Fill each mini bell pepper half with a spoonful of assorted seafood salad fillings.
2. Arrange the stuffed mini bell peppers on a serving platter.
3. Garnish with fresh herbs for added flavor and visual appeal.
4. Serve the seafood salad stuffed mini bell peppers as a colorful and bite-sized appetizer option for entertaining.

These seafood salad recipes are perfect for entertaining guests, offering a variety of creative and elegant options for any gathering. Whether it's the impressive Seafood Charcuterie Board, the interactive Seafood Salad Platter with Dipping Sauces, the flavorful Seafood Salad Skewers with Citrus Glaze, or the adorable Seafood Salad Stuffed Mini Bell Peppers, these dishes are sure to impress and delight your guests at any event or party!

Chapter (17) Seafood Salad Dressing DIY

A. Homemade Thousand Island Dressing
Ingredients:

- 1/2 cup mayonnaise
- 2 tablespoons ketchup
- 1 tablespoon sweet pickle relish
- 1 teaspoon white vinegar
- 1/2 teaspoon Worcestershire sauce
- Salt and pepper, to taste

Instructions:

1. In a bowl, combine mayonnaise, ketchup, sweet pickle relish, white vinegar, and Worcestershire sauce.
2. Mix well until all ingredients are fully incorporated.
3. Season with salt and pepper to taste.
4. Adjust the consistency by adding a little more mayonnaise or vinegar if desired.
5. Use immediately or refrigerate until ready to use. Stir before serving.

B. Lemon Herb Yogurt Dressing
Ingredients:

- 1/2 cup plain Greek yogurt
- 2 tablespoons fresh lemon juice
- 1 tablespoon olive oil
- 1 tablespoon chopped fresh herbs (such as parsley, dill, or chives)
- 1 teaspoon honey (optional)
- Salt and pepper, to taste

Instructions:

1. In a bowl, whisk together Greek yogurt, fresh lemon juice, olive oil, chopped fresh herbs, and honey (if using).
2. Season with salt and pepper to taste.
3. Adjust the consistency by adding a little more lemon juice or olive oil if desired.
4. Use immediately or refrigerate until ready to use. Stir before serving.

C. Tangy Honey Mustard Dressing
Ingredients:

- 1/4 cup Dijon mustard
- 2 tablespoons honey
- 2 tablespoons apple cider vinegar
- 1/4 cup olive oil
- Salt and pepper, to taste

Instructions:

1. In a bowl, whisk together Dijon mustard, honey, and apple cider vinegar until well combined.
2. Slowly drizzle in olive oil while whisking continuously to emulsify the dressing.
3. Season with salt and pepper to taste.
4. Adjust the sweetness or tanginess by adding more honey or vinegar if desired.
5. Use immediately or refrigerate until ready to use. Stir before serving.

D. Spicy Mango Lime Dressing
Ingredients:

- 1 ripe mango, peeled and diced
- 2 tablespoons lime juice
- 1 tablespoon honey or agave nectar
- 1 teaspoon grated ginger
- 1/4 teaspoon chili powder (adjust to taste)
- Salt, to taste

Instructions:

1. In a blender or food processor, combine diced mango, lime juice, honey or agave nectar, grated ginger, chili powder, and a pinch of salt.
2. Blend until smooth and creamy.
3. Adjust the consistency by adding a little water if needed.
4. Taste and adjust the sweetness, acidity, and spiciness according to your preference by adding more honey, lime juice, or chili powder.
5. Use immediately or refrigerate until ready to use. Stir before serving.

These homemade seafood salad dressings offer a variety of flavors to complement your favorite seafood salads. Whether it's the classic tanginess of Thousand Island Dressing, the refreshing zest of Lemon Herb Yogurt Dressing, the sweet and tangy notes of Tangy Honey Mustard Dressing, or the exotic kick of Spicy Mango Lime Dressing, these DIY dressings will elevate your seafood salads to a whole new level of deliciousness!

Chapter (18) Seafood Salad Preservation and Canning

A. Pickled Shrimp Salad
Ingredients:

- 1 lb (450g) cooked shrimp, peeled and deveined
- 1 cup apple cider vinegar
- 1/4 cup water
- 2 tablespoons sugar
- 1 teaspoon salt
- 1 teaspoon mustard seeds
- 1 teaspoon whole peppercorns
- 2 bay leaves
- 1 small red onion, thinly sliced
- 2 cloves garlic, minced
- Fresh dill, chopped (optional)

Instructions:

1. In a saucepan, combine apple cider vinegar, water, sugar, salt, mustard seeds, peppercorns, and bay leaves. Bring to a simmer over medium heat, stirring until sugar and salt dissolve.
2. Remove the brine from heat and let it cool completely.
3. In sterilized jars, layer cooked shrimp, sliced red onion, minced garlic, and chopped fresh dill (if using).
4. Pour the cooled brine over the shrimp mixture, ensuring all ingredients are submerged.
5. Seal the jars tightly and refrigerate for at least 24 hours before serving.
6. Serve the pickled shrimp salad as a tangy and flavorful appetizer or topping for salads and sandwiches.

B. Canned Tuna Salad with Herbs
Ingredients:

- 2 cans (5 oz each) tuna, drained
- 1/4 cup mayonnaise
- 2 tablespoons chopped fresh herbs (such as parsley, dill, or chives)
- 1 tablespoon lemon juice
- Salt and pepper, to taste

Instructions:

1. In a bowl, mix together drained tuna, mayonnaise, chopped fresh herbs, lemon juice, salt, and pepper until well combined.
2. Spoon the tuna salad into sterilized canning jars, leaving some headspace.
3. Wipe the jar rims with a clean cloth, then seal the jars with sterilized lids and rings.
4. Process the jars in a boiling water bath for the appropriate time according to your altitude (typically 90 minutes for pint jars).
5. Once processed, carefully remove the jars from the water bath and let them cool completely before storing in a cool, dark place.
6. Serve the canned tuna salad with herbs as a convenient and protein-packed meal option.

C. Smoked Salmon Salad Jars
Ingredients:

- 8 oz smoked salmon, flaked
- 1 cup Greek yogurt
- 2 tablespoons chopped fresh dill
- 1 tablespoon lemon juice
- 1 teaspoon Dijon mustard

- Salt and pepper, to taste
- Mixed salad greens
- Cherry tomatoes, halved
- Cucumber, sliced
- Red onion, thinly sliced
- Lemon wedges

Instructions:

1. In a bowl, mix together flaked smoked salmon, Greek yogurt, chopped fresh dill, lemon juice, Dijon mustard, salt, and pepper until well combined.
2. Layer the smoked salmon mixture and mixed salad greens in sterilized canning jars.
3. Top with halved cherry tomatoes, sliced cucumber, and thinly sliced red onion.
4. Seal the jars tightly and refrigerate until ready to serve.
5. Serve the smoked salmon salad jars with lemon wedges for a refreshing and nutritious meal option.

D. Preserved Crab and Corn Salad
Ingredients:

- 1 lb (450g) lump crabmeat, picked over for shells
- 1 cup corn kernels (fresh or frozen)
- 1/2 cup diced red bell pepper
- 1/4 cup chopped fresh cilantro
- 2 tablespoons apple cider vinegar
- 1 tablespoon olive oil
- 1 tablespoon honey
- Salt and pepper, to taste

Instructions:

1. In a bowl, combine lump crabmeat, corn kernels, diced red bell pepper, and chopped fresh cilantro.
2. In a small saucepan, whisk together apple cider vinegar, olive oil, honey, salt, and pepper over medium heat until well combined.
3. Pour the vinegar mixture over the crab and corn mixture and toss gently to coat.
4. Spoon the preserved crab and corn salad into sterilized canning jars, leaving some headspace.
5. Wipe the jar rims with a clean cloth, then seal the jars with sterilized lids and rings.
6. Process the jars in a boiling water bath for the appropriate time according to your altitude (typically 15 minutes for half-pint jars).
7. Once processed, carefully remove the jars from the water bath and let them cool completely before storing in a cool, dark place.
8. Serve the preserved crab and corn salad as a delightful and versatile dish for salads, sandwiches, or appetizers.

These preserved seafood salad recipes allow you to enjoy your favorite seafood dishes for longer periods, whether it's the tangy Pickled Shrimp Salad, the flavorful Canned Tuna Salad with Herbs, the convenient Smoked Salmon Salad Jars, or the versatile Preserved Crab and Corn Salad. Enjoy the convenience of having these delicious seafood salads ready to enjoy whenever you desire!

Chapter (19) Seafood Salad Garnishes and Toppings

A. Crispy Shallots and Garlic Chips
Ingredients:

- Shallots, thinly sliced
- Garlic cloves, thinly sliced
- Vegetable oil for frying
- Salt

Instructions:

1. Heat vegetable oil in a small saucepan over medium heat.
2. Fry the thinly sliced shallots and garlic in batches until golden brown and crispy, about 2-3 minutes.
3. Remove the crispy shallots and garlic chips from the oil using a slotted spoon and transfer them to a paper towel-lined plate to drain excess oil.
4. Season with salt while still hot.
5. Sprinkle the crispy shallots and garlic chips over seafood salads just before serving for added texture and flavor.

B. Toasted Coconut Flakes
Ingredients:

- Unsweetened coconut flakes

Instructions:

1. Preheat the oven to 325°F (160°C).
2. Spread unsweetened coconut flakes in a single layer on a baking

sheet.

3. Bake in the preheated oven for 5-7 minutes, stirring occasionally, until golden brown and fragrant.
4. Remove from the oven and let the toasted coconut flakes cool completely.
5. Sprinkle the toasted coconut flakes over seafood salads for a nutty and crunchy topping.

C. Candied Lemon Zest
Ingredients:

- Lemon zest strips (from 1-2 lemons)
- 1/2 cup granulated sugar
- 1/4 cup water

Instructions:

1. In a small saucepan, combine granulated sugar and water over medium heat, stirring until the sugar dissolves.
2. Add lemon zest strips to the sugar syrup and simmer for 10-15 minutes, until the zest strips become translucent.
3. Use a slotted spoon to transfer the candied lemon zest strips to a wire rack to cool and dry.
4. Once cooled and dried, finely chop the candied lemon zest.
5. Sprinkle the candied lemon zest over seafood salads for a sweet and citrusy garnish.

D. Pickled Red Onions and Radishes
Ingredients:

- Red onions, thinly sliced
- Radishes, thinly sliced
- 1 cup apple cider vinegar
- 1/2 cup water

- 2 tablespoons sugar
- 1 teaspoon salt

Instructions:

1. In a small saucepan, combine apple cider vinegar, water, sugar, and salt over medium heat, stirring until the sugar and salt dissolve.
2. Place thinly sliced red onions and radishes in a glass jar or bowl.
3. Pour the hot vinegar mixture over the sliced onions and radishes, ensuring they are fully submerged.
4. Let the pickled onions and radishes cool to room temperature, then cover and refrigerate for at least 1 hour before serving.
5. Drain the pickled onions and radishes before using as a tangy and colorful topping for seafood salads.

These garnishes and toppings add texture, flavor, and visual appeal to seafood salads. Whether it's the crispy shallots and garlic chips for a savory crunch, the toasted coconut flakes for a nutty accent, the candied lemon zest for a sweet citrus touch, or the pickled red onions and radishes for a tangy bite, these additions elevate the presentation and taste of your seafood creations.

Chapter (20) Seafood Salad and Wine Pairings

A. Chardonnay and Shrimp Salad

Chardonnay, with its rich and buttery notes, pairs wonderfully with shrimp salad. The creamy texture and subtle sweetness of Chardonnay complement the delicate flavor of shrimp without overwhelming it. Opt for a lightly oaked Chardonnay to enhance the salad's richness without dominating its flavors.

B. Sauvignon Blanc and Crab Salad

Sauvignon Blanc's crisp acidity and refreshing citrus notes make it an excellent match for crab salad. The wine's zesty character helps cleanse the palate after each bite of crab, while its herbal undertones add complexity to the pairing. Look for a Sauvignon Blanc from New Zealand or California for vibrant fruit flavors that enhance the salad's freshness.

C. Pinot Grigio and Tuna Salad

The light and crisp profile of Pinot Grigio pairs beautifully with tuna salad. Its citrusy notes and subtle floral aromas complement the mild flavor of tuna, while its refreshing acidity cuts through any richness in the salad. Choose a Pinot Grigio from Italy or Oregon for its bright acidity and clean finish, enhancing the flavors of the tuna salad.

D. Rosé and Lobster Salad

Rosé, with its delicate fruitiness and refreshing acidity, is a versatile choice for lobster salad. Its vibrant flavors of red berries and stone fruits provide a lovely contrast to the richness of lobster, while its crisp finish keeps the palate cleansed. Opt for a dry Provence Rosé or a light-bodied Rosé from California for an elegant pairing that highlights the salad's flavors.

❖ Conclusion: Dive into the World of Seafood Salads

A. Final Thoughts

Seafood salads offer a world of flavors, textures, and culinary possibilities that are both delicious and nutritious. From classic recipes to creative twists, regional variations to vegetarian alternatives, there's something for every palate to explore and enjoy. By incorporating fresh seafood, vibrant vegetables, and flavorful dressings, you can create salads that are light and refreshing or rich and indulgent, perfect for any occasion.

B. Encouragement for Culinary Exploration

As you embark on your culinary journey with seafood salads, don't be afraid to experiment and innovate. Explore different ingredients, flavor combinations, and presentation styles to create your own signature dishes. Whether you're hosting a dinner party, packing a picnic, or simply enjoying a weeknight meal, seafood salads offer endless opportunities for creativity and culinary expression.

C. Invitation to Share Feedback and Recipes

We would love to hear about your experiences with seafood salads and any recipes you've tried or created. Your feedback and insights are invaluable in helping us continue to develop and refine our culinary repertoire. Feel free to share your thoughts, suggestions, and recipes with us, as we strive to inspire and delight fellow seafood enthusiasts around the world.

Thank you for joining us on this journey into the world of seafood salads. We hope you've discovered new flavors, found inspiration for your next culinary adventure, and enjoyed the diverse array of recipes presented. Here's to many more delicious seafood salads in your future!